Advance Praise

Risa Denenberg's *Whirlwind @ Lesbos* is a collection chronicling one life echoed in many lives, real and imagined: girlhood loves, activism, friendships ravaged by AIDS, a lover lost to suicide, a son lost to a custody battle, the body getting old, the heart congesting. Women's voices speak across time and place, but are all bound by the same fierce desires, the same heartaches. *Whirlwind @ Lesbos* is a decisively erotic, explicitly lesbian collection, where the speaker being entered by a lover feels herself to be "a glove/surrounding her like a galaxy." But even the intensity of passion is tinged by melancholy, a sense of separateness. "I am no more alone than Emily Dickinson," notes the speaker, as if that fragile link to the most isolated of women poets might provide a measure of comfort. These poems are written at a distance from the speaker's passionate early self, recalling with a sense of astonishment the time "When I was still trying/to undress the universe/and know her." That time is no more. "And that has been my story," says the speaker ruefully in another poem, "not her face/but my hapless life." Yet despite a life punctuated by pain and loss, these are proud, tender and passionate poems, recounted unflinchingly, with acute lyric intensity.

@ RACHEL ROSE

"I wanted more of those nights/ your wild fingers inside me": stately yet vulnerable, these poems are vibrant reports of humans wrestling with that icky thing, baggage— sometimes lost, sometimes stolen, never forgotten. Full of passions marked by place, but not by boundaries, *Whirlwind @ Lesbos* is a necessary collection in our contemporary era of shoved-away storage units and international border politics.

@ AMY KING

Risa Denenberg's *Whirlwind @ Lesbos* is a fine coming-of-age collection especially relatable to women who evolved during the 70s and 80s and discovered woman love. Spare and sensual, the poems embody the struggle with yearning, loss, and acceptance. Confronting the complexity of physical desire and how it wanes with age, these poems leave the reader wanting to read them again and again. They are the real stuff—emotional heart and power.

@ CHELLA COURINGTON

Risa Denenberg's *Whirlwind @ Lesbos* is a book of life lived, the sense we have when older that this, here, now, is all epilogue. Denenberg recalls the thrill of young love, or was it love imagined, or love in history books, or myth? They run together, overlap, through echoes of Sappho 31, "He seems to me equal to the gods," the lover who can bear proximity to the beloved without implosion. Now, though, when spring returns, / the forsythia fail to astonish. As sure as I know the anhedonia of which Denenberg speaks, I know these poems are a pleasure.

@ MICHAEL H. BRODER

Whirlwind

@

Lesbos

Whirlwind

@

Lesbos

Risa Denenberg

Headmistress Press

ISBN-13: 978-0692739563
ISBN-10: 0692739564

Cover art © 2002 by Patricia Cronin. *Memorial To A Marriage,* Carrara marble, over life-size. Photo courtesy the artist. Back cover photo by Este Gardner of Risa Denenberg, 1974.

Cover & book design by Mary Meriam.

PUBLISHER
Headmistress Press
60 Shipview Lane
Sequim, WA 98382
Telephone: 917-428-8312
Email: headmistresspress@gmail.com
Website: headmistresspress.blogspot.com

With gratitude
to poets, mentors, editors, friends
and especially, to Headmistress Press.

Contents

@

Whirlwind @ Lesbos   1

@@

So,   5
Femme Leaves Home   6
I didn't want to marry you   8
for girls who fuck like sisters   9
Her Particularity   11
Butches and Bed Death   12
Her Ambivalence   13
(unavailable)   14
Study in Desire   16
Pierce Me with Feathers   17
I remember your face   18
The converse of desire   19
For all I know,   20
Perfect Reader   21
Raspberry Jam   22
About the body and what it needs   23

@@@

Eating the Seed Corn   27

@@@@

Anhedonia   35
After the Dentist   36

Black Moon   37
Rachel, Rachel   38
History of Fragments   39
Malignant Dream   40

@@@@@

Slight   43
After the Affair   44
A Mere Shudder   45
Avocado, sideways   46
The last time   47
at the end   48
Wild speaks to me in Dervish   49

@@@@@@

Score   53
Arrhythmia   54
Gesture   55
This is Heartbreak   56

Acknowledgments   59

Whirlwind @ Lesbos

We met in Istanbul
where your face was a veil
and you beckoned a reckless gesture.

Cover your eyes, you hissed
when I dared look through
your robe at your breast buds.

You were twelve when we first kissed
wadded your gum under the desk
whistled at me, spit into the wind
earnestly began chewing my hair.

We ran away to Naples
during the long war while flames
licked our feet and charred our skin.

Hurry, you barked over your shoulder
I was already losing sight.

I wailed all night in Jerusalem
when you turned me hard
against the stone wall
pressing against my back
as your reached up inside me
grabbed my womb with your fist.

In winter, we rented a small cottage
in Copenhagen where winds blew
snow over our bed
we embraced and couldn't let go
you were cold and needed comfort.

We undressed each other
maidens in the fifth century
and were discovered naked
entwined asleep
your ringlets black and soft
on the silken pillow.

But then I missed the cab to the airport
slept right through the alarm
one morning in Cairo
and you were gone.

I was beheaded
with your name on my lips.

The baggage was clearly marked
but reached Paris by error.

I'm in New York
awaiting your email.

So,

my mind was leaving for California the next day
without prospects for job or roof or bed
just fleeing, having had enough
of whatever it was I was looking for but not finding in Seattle
when, in a flash, I was at a dinner party
with 2 women, then 6 women, a whole cabal of women
with little cone hats and a cake, some bubbly, and later
someone had to walk me home in reverse, I'd lost my way
and my shirt had come undone
and there was a kiss, chaste, and I shut the door
afraid of more

Femme Leaves Home

Do you miss having
feta cheese omelets
in the morning,
and fried potatoes?

Do you miss me at all
or just my things,
my activities, what I did
for you, the sense that I
belonged there?

Did you hate the idea
of family, of taking care
of each other—was it
too bourgeois for you
did it slap your revolutionary
ideals, undermine your
radical vision?

Did I remind you
of someone you hate
or can't stand
to be around, did I
harm you?

Was my domesticity
too much for your feminism
did you feel more
comfortable apportioning
chores—complaining about
who didn't clean the bathroom?

Was fucking me
one of those chores?

Is there any sense
of loss here—of torn
garments or fractured
bones, of mirrors covered
in black cloth?

Do you think of me only
as a woman who bakes,
who fries, who burns,
who stews in her own juices?

I didn't want to marry you

I only wanted more of those nights
where we ate pizza or omelets
I wanted more of those nights
your wild fingers inside me
nights where we shared
a pint of ice cream
I wanted more
for me

I didn't want
to cry like this
I only wanted more
of those nights where we sang
at the top of our range, read tarot
went around the corner to shoot pool
eat Mexican food, drink a margarita

I only wanted more of those nights
when you told me your dreams
or mentioned your mother
when you fucked me
or pulled my hand
around your
waist

I never
wanted vows
asked for public notices
tried on wedding gowns
I never asked for changes of residence
I only wanted another night next to you in bed
just brief relief from wondering who you're fucking now

for girls who fuck like sisters

they were it
girl fuck-buddies
best friends
who could fuck each other
and anyone else they pleased

never treading on jealously
living together effortlessly
without heat, without rancor
roommates in college
with boyfriends on the side
who snuggle up together
share shameful secrets

anticipate twenty or thirty
years of reunions
where they would laugh hard
at their girl exploits
enjoy the image they'd projected

best friends only want what's best for each other
are prepared for friendship
to terminate when significant others
arrive to take over
never feel bruised when it occurs
in fact, are thrilled

ready to be a bridesmaid
at a moment's notice
always know just
what to wear

are never caught naked
can accept reality, and
at the reception's end
a kiss to the cheek is most acceptable

and, darling
shall we make a date
one year from now
pour scotch over rocks
and catch up on old times?

Her Particularity

Her ordinary white cotton briefs.
The way she gulped coffee in the morning, cheeks puffed out
        slightly, before swallowing.
How she missed her drinking buddy Patrick.
Her early hunger for my body: *I can't stop.*
Kitchen burns in various stages of healing on her hands and wrists.
AIDS funerals on her birthday two years in a row.
The way it felt to hear her say: *Come here.*
The Irish Pub where she told me about the affair.
The way she could extinguish the past.
Small details of her vocabulary: *Could you rub my back?*
        Five more minutes? Please?
The story of her father's sanguine appearance at the dinner table
        the night before he died.
Her memory, age eleven, saying to her mother, *he's getting better,*
        isn't he?
What she said after telling me about the affair: *I'm sorry.*
The affront of the affair-bitch answering her phone.
The agony of two sessions of couples' counseling.
What she said when I begged her to stop:
The tough-tender way she taught homeless women culinary skills,
        as if history could be set free.

Butches and Bed Death

One of her early lines:
I've always wanted a relationship
where the sex didn't end.

What she promised:
I'll make love to you this weekend.
I promise.

What she said after we stopped
having sex: *I don't really think*
it helps to talk about it.

Her final answer:
I don't know.
I guess I just don't want to.

How I still feel for her:
I adore her.
I'd go back to her in a heartbeat.

Why:
I'm not saying.
Too many girls are after her already.

Her Ambivalence

Her hand enchants as it enters
finger by finger. I am a glove
surrounding her like a galaxy.

Only her mouth rejects me:
I can't get any work done
with you here.

When I cry in pain or pleasure,
she stuffs a section of orange
into my mouth. She invites me

to dine amidst clutter, dragging
a toothbrush back and forth.
Her hands silently deliver

their promise, precise and steady.
But where to put my tongue when
she sends me home?

She wants this to be easy, facile.
I only understand it when it's hard.

(unavailable)

(I'm awake at five in the morning
with a vivid recollection
of that drunken) kiss

the hot sense of
your possible opening to me
has become a silent rerun

(much later you tell me
you have a girlfriend)

we are spent with sweaty
after-sex in some scenery-less
colorless bedroom

(why don't I hear you
saying no?)

there are tons of these
suggested moments, edges
which seem sharp and real

(your intentions
are unknown to me)

shall I surprise you
press myself upon
your untidy landscape
without so much as a phone call

(which is less offensive—a sly
affair or an open imbroglio?)

since I have noticed your heat
as a possibility
I can't confine my urge
to scratch you

(you are ready for something
but not disclosure)

you don't deny
the ripe dialog, the intensity
that fires thick air
between us

(say something)

or stop me with your tongue

Study in Desire

I consider wanting you
but then, won't you just become
another passing fancy?

For now, you're a reflection,
elbows resting on the bar
sipping a Becks, casually

exposing an edge of breast.
I think about wanting you
and how you could hurt me.

Would we practice alienation
or merely inertia? I scan
the odds, try to feel nothing.

But then, it happens.
The dam bursts
and we go flooding

down unfamiliar streets
lacking rules or manners
until the distraction

of ample sex drops us roughly
and abruptly down on the day
you begin to refuse me simple

civility. And you will leave me
pondering why I plumb
the dank terrains of desire.

Pierce Me with Feathers

When I was a biddy, I carved notches along the length
of my thigh and a half moon above my breast.

For you. For years, I hovered on my perch, waiting
for your return, without hope or prospect of reward.

I've savored young flappers adorned with their plumes.
And now you dare tease with these cheap titbits?

My scars are wasp stingers lodged in tender
flesh. I once fancied you, but love is sly as a hawk.

Fly away damn bluebird, you aren't the bird of paradise,
you're no better than any other chick. I do not starve,

yet remain ravenous. The sex we had back then
left no keepsake in my gullet, nor wings to fly.

I remember your face

Grinning up at me as I toppled you, us
upon a worn Moroccan bed/spread
under a South Miami sky, Cassiopeia
above, hemmed in by the sickly-sweet
surfeit of gardenia bushes that barely hid
our flaunt, after that first kiss, my first
woman-kiss, yours too.

                                Thinking the grin
involved something akin to solidarity,
both of us sleeping with the same man,
no longer my man but not yours either,
so this extracurricular cheating
seemed worth a great deal that night.

I can't remember your name.
Five decades of weather have
dampened the celebration.

The converse of desire

Her succulent face, so full
        of something I can't fathom, I want to dash
into her arms, but can't, those lips stop me,
        lavish and candied, like yams or bubblegum blown
to near-pop, and when she looks at me, I die,
        I absolutely die in place because I am so taken
with her charm that it shrills my tongue
        and makes me shudder, a deep full shudder
that takes over my breathing and muddles my brain.

        And that has been my story, not her face,
but my hapless life, a life in which I refuse
        to meet anyone's gaze with affection,
in which I turn away, rather than dash into arms,
        arms that should hold, but can't.

For all I know,

you may be in an alleyway shooting
heroin, or maybe you just got tired of my malady.
No call, no message, no nada.

The last time you gazed into my eyes
the firmament lit up and shooting stars grazed
my face, my body splayed out on pillows, ready.

Yours is the gaze of an infant at breast, the gawk
of a groupie flashing skin, the glare of a stern judge
who doles out the punishing love I so crave.

What sin did I commit? What wrong
have I done to be left so bereft? How many labors
must I perform to win you back?

Perfect Reader

After a dreamy recital, she stands
at the podium, disposed to take
a few questions.

Someone asks: *Who is your ideal reader?*
Modestly, she replies, *One who reads
a poem more than once.*

There and then, I vow to be her reader.
I will recite the poem until its words enter me
like a lover who waits for the silky readiness
of the beloved's lust.

I will read aloud and in silence, I will memorize
line by line. I will read ardently and get lost
time and again. I will backstroke languidly
to the beginning a million times
to locate, not her meaning, nor mine,
but ours.

Or if there is no meaning, I will
contemplate the depths of emptiness.
I will not be deterred by difficult diction
or syntax. I will chew the poem
down to its scaffolding and ink it with
red stars to navigate each of its turns.

I will not sleep or eat
during the countless hours
of our tête-á-tête.

Raspberry Jam

It's maraschino red,
so red you can't help but think
it's insincere. Reminds me of ketchup
in Copenhagen, perfect foil for those Danish
sausages that astonished with chubby flavor. Or
the blood of afterbirth. This jam, in its tiny rectangle,
reminds me of the Sunflour Cafe in Seattle and the enormous
affection I reserve for breakfast. And tragically, it reminds me
of you in Miami, wet from shower in ruby robe.

About the body and what it needs

I navigate by shadows of clouds in the ocean.
I don't need a mother or lover to enter my vessel,
or to amend legends that were never mine.

I don't recall labor pains, but still feel the rush
of milk tumble into empty breasts — a small shiver
of memory that sates longing, leaves me engorged.

You must wonder how I say these things that seem
so faded. In full sight of your fraught wish to be loved
in body, my rebuff must affront you.

I will not be coy: I know it does. Since,
if these things about me were not true,
I could foist the love you seek upon you.

I am no more alone than Emily Dickinson.
There is no idiom for the seasonal way I sail
into myself. The clouds are blue today.

Eating the Seed Corn

It's 2011.

I think stating the year is important although
it's often omitted. February flight from Seattle
to Boston: snow strewn across the belly of a nation,
geography dotted with symbols, jotting short
in-flight word-strings on college-lined pages

in a composition notebook with marble-blue cover.
Reading *Mean Free Path* where *B* says: *don't take my voice,*
or some such. Maybe: *hold these thoughts like cupcakes.*
Time feels virtual, but my heart is corporeal. So I go back
to the foreword to find: *don't throw my voice away.*

Not a womanly idiom, although *B* has sampled
the contour and clothing of a woman. Shall I surmise:
a man throws, a woman takes? Still, I prefer stillness.
Until she strapped it on and entered me (1978) I couldn't
predicate, although I dreamt (and this is a point—

on my actual birthday—but which one?) that she
dumped me down a garbage chute, walking
arm-in-arm with another. That summer, my heart
could pump, and I felt nothing, puppy love. Compare
it to the awful love that weighs me now. Sorry

I didn't care about your orgasm and couldn't fake it.
B, thank God you have your A. I've told anyone who
would listen. I was born sanguine, what year did I
turn liverish? When did my heart congest? I opt
to live alone. You don't believe it when I tell you

my life is drawing to a close. Even those who long
to believe in an afterlife know it's only a wild card.
I recognize dust when it settles on furniture. What
can it mean that I fell in love with a lean volume
of poems? How to express gratitude to a font

of intertextuality? That I felt its wind enter my anima
and cause my veneer to burst open? Can we ever
wholly stake our claims to each other? What sort
of mother wants to make her daughter feel inadequate?
She insisted to have said nothing of the sort. Perhaps

I misconstrued and turned left instead of right,
stumbled upon a life I never should have known.
Now I take medicine apart and find its wings, hidden
under the carapace thorax. The group interview
for the PhD program @ NYU (1997), when my mother's

illness beckoned like a siren, my heart blocked,
these deans and professors an anchor to the city.
What did the question signify? I wore a dress,
the next-to-last time. Could you unpack it please?
Winds blew me up and down the I-95 corridor from NYC

to Silver Spring every weekend, but I forged my way back.
I never could arrive because distance cannot be reduced
by more than half. On my 50th birthday (2000) I wore
an ankle-length Chinese shift, having dinner with 8 friends
at a place in the East Village called

But this was a short smoky A-line jersey from the GAP,
worn with a fetching red sweater. One professor asked,
Isn't this a bit like War and Peace? And because I had
never read W&P, I hung my hat, gathered my books,
and retreated from delusions of academia. I wore black

silk to my mother's funeral (2001); *that* was the last time.
It's just that my heart is bigger now, flabbier, and I look
lousy in dresses. Do not bury me in a gown, please. Do
not bury me at all, leave me on a rock for the vultures,
burn me in the pyre, eat my ash-torn flesh with your hands.

Do what you wish with the body, me being the dead.
Make me your home, turtle-shell. I've told anyone who
would listen. After the third breakup, you don't show
your face. Standing at the front of the room with the
women at ACT UP NY meetings at the Gay and Lesbian

Community Center, 14th Street, Monday nights (1988-1994),
those lesbians and gay boys sleeping together—what
moxie! I came to New York (1988) seeking sex and left
celibate (2006). My best friend *J* died at St. Vincent's
Hospital in the West Village (1993). Before he stopped

speaking he was light enough to carry from bed to bath.
His last words to me were: *Shut up R.* Some said we
were like an old married couple. But we weren't old
and the bitterness of his dying shrouded everything.
Now (2011) my heart is weak and my aging ugliness

appalls me, I don't wish to look. He repeatedly
instructed us to burn his body in the street and eat
his flesh. I put a bit of his ashes in the coleslaw, six
of us reciting Mourner's Kaddish one year later (1994)
on the beach at Cherry Grove—*N, C, J, B,* &

It's hard to remember names if you don't write them down.
Location is also relevant. The spaces we can't see, tiny
metrics between electrons, their loneliness, our distance.
I can't imagine the heart that once loved him. We fear
what is unknown: cloudy eyes that see but do not see;

hair so dry, skin so oily; strange food, unfamiliar textures,
wanton tastes, odorless gases. A boy sitting next to you
on the school bus slyly inserting finger, where? Did
it happen in the bathroom? Was it a short story? I have
not forgotten *B* or *J* or any of my infatuations, not even

my first boyfriend *D* (1964) who years later (2004)
told me I reminded him of a cat—amusing and fickle.
My first woman-lover *L* (1975) committed suicide. I want you
to know how much this means to me, but have no way
to tell you. I'm afraid I will die without discovering how

it plays out, without remembering to burn my journals.
We are in such a hurry, running out of time, snacking
on seed corn. From the periodic table I take carbon,
oxygen, nephron. I have a friend who is blind but reads
via absence of vision, substance of clouds or cloudy

lenses sharpening her lens to foveal pointillism.
Everything arises from the uncertain arrangement
of electrons, their locations—undisturbed, unseen.
Everything we know is matter, everything we feel
is light waves. All the words are wrong, they are fictions,

sucking the core, leaving the skin dry, lizard-like.
Although I never meant to tell you, when the leaves
turn next time, I will leave you. Although I tell you often,
you don't listen. Although you don't believe in God
or angels, the blank of blanks, I will leave you. I never asked

your permission. I have forgotten my hungers, I am dry now,
prepared for the suffering and the emptying. I have made
certain promises, but only to myself. You've asked
for my story, and I shan't disclose any puny miracles.
Why start with birth when death is so much more

compelling? Yes, I delivered my son *M* (1969), squatting
on a sleeping bag at the Noor Hotel, Kabul, Afghanistan.
There, now I've said it. Make of it what you will.
If you are seeking your one-and-only, I don't think
you will ever be sure. There will always be a nugget

of doubt. Biological tickles, mutations, gingivitis.
Is there something beneath the pattern? Could you
remove the patina, unearth the primal cave drawings?
We mean nothing if not what we mean. The old are young
forever, learning the longhand view of epochs and dynasties,

dinosaurs and the Garden of *E*. Flashes of insight
like hydrogen bombs, craters of nameless damage
reaching the surface breath by breath, floating bodies
dying. Already dead. Time does not ache for them.
I didn't know you could so easily discard me while

I waited patiently for you. I begged you not to lead me on,
if you weren't going to stop seeing her. Then you said:
I haven't stopped. I won't. Time is coming fast. Hard
to ignore relativity. It's noon in Seattle, 3 in Boston.
View from the train window, roaming North on the Amtrak

Downeaster, Boston to Portland, trees fly by at different
speeds depending on their distance. Time is space,
I can see this with my own eyes, even at this age
of failing sight, even with hearing loss, I try to hear
between the lies. A quarter-century of hypertension.

My father's mother's apoplexy (1935). Four drugs.
Will it work? Incant: *Please, please, please.* There
are mending words in the air. They are free. Clip
them like coupons. I should plant rows of corn seeds
before I die, leave something for my grandsons,

my brother's children, that future we hate
to acknowledge—the one without us. I can see
how this is going, read the handwritten progress
notes, taste the stale bread, smell the twice-brewed
coffee. I'll need to hurry if I'm to get all the chores

done. It's 2011. *When will I have the stroke?*

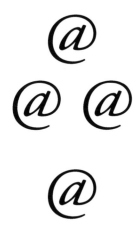

Anhedonia

I have no talent for pleasure.
My skin rebuffs touch. Plunking
through weeks of days, the music
goes *bleep, bleep, bleep.* Even the sea
has lost its brine. Ticking off senses
one by one as they wither. Spring returns,
the forsythia fail to astonish.

I once loved long morning drives
along winding country roads,
as the sun swelled centimeter
by centimeter through seasons,
until for one week, a blinding blaze,
and then its pale retreat. Wondering
what happens to fields of corn stalks
turned under, leaves that drain green
to reveal bursts of orange, delight
at winter's first snow.

When I was still trying
to undress the universe
and know her.

After the Dentist

I step into a lusterless bistro and order oysters.
I'm always wishing people would just shut up.
It's 2:45 and I was foolishly hoping to be alone.

Passing thoughts are couplets uncaptured, run
aground by conversations I've no choice but to catch.
I'm a spoiled sort in a chattering world.

But let me now unruffle my tail feathers. I want
a quiet that tastes like slices of lemon floating
on arctic sea. When the waitress doesn't bring bread,

I don't eat bread. I'm not interested in intercourse.
I lost custody of my son when he was barely five.
I've learned to do without.

I always return to the written word. It lasts longer
and leaves a better trace. I'm not lost out here
in my small craft. I'm writing, not lonely.

Black Moon

I knew nothing until I fell from the handlebars of your bicycle, onto a world of stones. As this will be our last descent, I'll soon hide beneath the bed and play dead. You'll find only socks and dust, my body blameless and invisible. A stain runs through the Book, each page a Rorschach of crimson-yellow. I wanted to see the prairie grass aflame, not fire engines blinking in the median strip, foiling traffic. The sod smolders when no one mourns for the unburnt. With bare soles, I interpret what's beneath—stone, loam, linoleum. I sleep on a straw mattress and eat only apples. I've kept *J's* amethyst ring lost on a Greyhound bus, my first studio in the East Village with its kitchen bathtub, a bottle of Seconal. My feet no longer reach the floor. Come now, if you wish to see me before another new moon fails to appear in the sky.

Rachel, Rachel

Grade school gives a loner nothing
to look forward to. Waiting for the bus, shivering
unseen, you shudder with unutterable lust—

while Mr. Sock Monkey and Lil' Miss No Name doze
in the toy box, begging you to come and play.
But it's too late to fake childliness. Too late
to pretend you're like the others. You lie in bed,
aquake with a torment you can't lay fingers on.

In 1968, when you saw the scenes in *Rachel, Rachel*
where Joanne Woodward scorns self-sex, rebukes
woman-kiss, barters with shame and hunger—
It's just so I can sleep, you knew exactly
what she craved.

History of Fragments

A few precise memories: Yellow stepstool,
attic dormer where I grow secret breasts, kitchen
where Zayde places a lump of sugar between
rotten teeth and dissolves it with hot black tea
slurped from a jelly glass.

A legend: In the summer of '69, a man named Dwight
becomes paralyzed sitting in front of a Swanson
TV dinner and has to be taken to the mental ward.
He can't answer the question: *Do I like peas?*
Or not?

An unreliable narrator: Battered shack deep
in the North Florida panhandle, newborn swathed
in newspaper laid out on cold cement floor, not breathing.
A six-year old girl opens her mouth, but has no words
for what she sees. Her mother is mute.

A possible fact: In bed, I caress my earlobe, so soft.
So much like the pink satin edge on my
transitional-object blankie, sucking my thumb,
sucking, sucking, sucking, until mother
paints it with foul-tasting syrup.

A query: More and more alone, I roam in circles,
play game after game of solitaire, eager to place
the 7 of hearts atop the 8 of hearts. I practice over
and over in my sleep. *Am I the girl he fondled?*

Malignant Dream

I dreamt my hair was silver
and my body thin—like a friend
who died last month of breast cancer.

Her hair turned
overnight it seemed,
luxuriant in its thick new growth,
body svelte
before vanishing.

So many have left me.

How often now
I long
for my turn.

Slight

Consider the girl with the pixie-cut black hair
in a crimson leather jacket who sits at the bar nursing
a beer. Set that image next to the chance that she might shove
her love into me with a glance. How such puny
slights foretold my fall from grace.

After the Affair

Back then, after the affair
when you went back to your girlfriend
and every cell of mine was still fully attuned
to your every phrase, each clumsy gesture,
while we were still living collectively
(some of us sleeping on pallets on a hardwood floor)
I might have asked something small of you,
Could we go to dinner, just us, please?

And sometimes you would agree.
We never did those things again, never ran off
together to tackle our horny stickiness
which, in my extremity, felt urgently
impossible. It was enough

if you said you would. To protect
what we'd had for a moment, which finally
was nothing but reckless longing. The kind
that might as well be attached to anything
or nothing at all.

A Mere Shudder

She imagines a long, lean body,
closes eyes as she gathers chubby hips,
laps at the salt lick of saggy tits,
tries to re-enter the rhythm and rhapsody,
the tango of limbs.

We make so much of this fickle
discharge of neurons—
this pling of electrical whim.

It takes such a rim of cunning
to maintain lust. A flower pot
of love-sick soup simmers
dimly on her back burners.

Avocado, sideways

As fog fastens the sky,
wind, yellow and garish,
batters the potted avocado tree on the porch

that sprung blind from the stone of store-bought fruit,
pinned with toothpicks, rigged upside down for weeks
in a shot glass of tap water.

I've begged
many a seed to breed
when it wouldn't.

I get close
only to plummet. Another way to fail
is to fall

like a tree in a squall
green-thin but tall
sprawling sideways.

The last time

The last time I lay with a woman—nuzzling,
fingering, nibbling, I felt nothing. I ran
all the clichéd fantasies I use—loathsome ones
I won't reveal, even the whimsy of Stevie Ray's
fat fingers working my strings. It's not fair
to lie in bed, but who hasn't?

After that, the earth tilted a few degrees leeward.
My body became a leper colony. Today I bring soup
to a neighbor who will die soon. Spooning broth
between her lips, I slip off shoes and climb
into bed with her.

at the end

no words were spoken, none heard
only the drone of breakers cresting and ebbing

the small child wedged between our hips could have been
drowning

you bobbed, I sank
your fury reeled
harder, meaner, swifter

I lunged, you churned
a syncopated hurricane
high winds shook the house
                        and blew walls away

no words spoken, none heard
I tumbled in as you washed ashore

Wild speaks to me in Dervish

Wild speaks in Dervish and flips me
like a crêpe. I hold my breath and wait
with the strain of wondering, *do I want it?*
And the frayed refrain, *why don't I want anymore?*

From God-view above,
the whirling makes a bit more sense—
like a tub full of freshly laundered angel wings
bleached to the brightest white that blind us
to green-black sludge in the drain.

My lust is a pounding headache
bound to a bundle of secrets
I won't be disclosing here. After the act,
I plead, *Wild, please leave, I need sleep.*

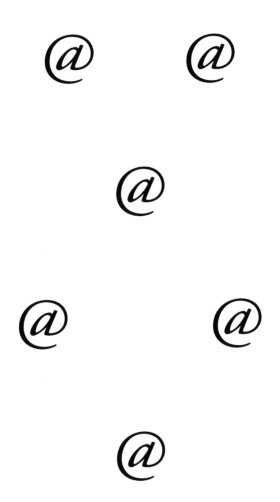

Score

She hoists the prize high above his head. He rises onto tiptoes,
lifts off the tarmac. Arms strain, shoulders sprout wings.
He would fly across the ocean to seal this pact.

Will she or won't she? She doesn't say—lupine mouth,
lipstick smile, seductive as a golden calf. Evading
his advances at the hoop, she scoops it higher, higher.

He grows—not fast enough, or too fast. Now she is down low,
a low-down dribbler, passing smoothly right between his legs.
She seals the answer in an envelope and hugs the berry-trophy

close to her chest. Burning through the night with the fever
of her knowledge, her body is a secret thing, an evil thing,
an unknown, unknowable, terrible thing.

Arrhythmia

Gasping, she lay down on the cool porcelain.
Storms tumbled over her. It took hours
to catch her breath, hoping for a vertex birth,
not imagining the tiny breech hand

                        that emerged.

She wondered what would happen next.
Was there enough strength to use forceps,
to tear the thing into parts?

She tried to sink into it,
the way the brain releases prolactin to let down
milk into breasts.

Could she forget that swan neck
and seraph wings? The glissade out of womb,
slipping through a midwife's sure hands across linoleum.

Rising from the tub, she shut the spigot.
In sudden silence, dread drummed its wild rhythm
inside her chest.

Gesture

I raised my hand to my forehead, scanning—
(I don't know what for, was it fever or despair?)

on hearing my father had died and, unable to reach
his body before its burial, I raised my hand

to my breast, thinking heartburn or infarction
and wept for him, for another, for all the corpses

but that was years ago, then I hear that yesterday
you raised your hand to your forehead

and collapsed, rushed by helicopter to Harborview
never knowing what for, was it stroke or lost hope

the scribbled note that fell into my lap at work
the call from a woman I've never met *(your friend)*

said, *taken off life support,* but the image of you—
the hand, the puzzled brow, the collapse, so vivid

but how did she know to call me, you and I
(can I say we?) had only just met, did she know

you had written a sonnet and sent it to me, as if
seeking my advice about poetry, until

(another hand-to-head moment) I realized it was
you, flirting, but instead of dinner or shy embrace

you are dead. Last night I dreamed our first kiss
our last kiss, as you darkly departed.

This is Heartbreak

I've squandered this vow mindlessly
scratching a sterile sore. The portents
were plain, nothing would come of it.

Still I dream. Last night, seven dead mice
strewn across the coverlet, harking back
to an arresting image—bodily harm—

rat emerging from vagina. I do not
make these things up, I'm too weary.
There is not enough salve

on the continent to swathe
this busted body, nor breath
to resuscitate this heartbreak.

Acknowledgments

Many thanks to the editors of the following publications, in which these poems appeared:

Amethyst: "Whirlwind @ Lesbos" (was "Whirlwind")

Arsenic Lobster: "Raspberry Jam"

Bay Windows: "Butches and Bed Death"

blinded by clouds (Hyacinth Girl Press, 2014): "Raspberry Jam," "at the end," and "Black Moon"

Common Lives, Lesbian Lives: "Femme Leaves Home"

Lavender Review: "So," and "About the body and what it needs"

Mean Distance from the Sun (Aldrich Press, 2013): "Malignant Dream" and "After the Dentist"

Menacing Hedge: "History of Fragments"

Mudlark: An Electronic Journal of Poetry and Poetics: "Eating the Seed Corn"

Permafrost: "Blackened Moon"

SoundZine: "Anhedonia," "Arrhythmia" and "This is Heartbreak"

The Writing Disorder: "Score"

Headmistress Press Books

Fireworks in the Graveyard - Joy Ladin
Social Dance - Carolyn Boll
The Force of Gratitude - Janice Gould
Spine - Sarah Caulfield
Diatribe from the Library - Farrell Greenwald Brenner
Blind Girl Grunt - Constance Merritt
Acid and Tender - Jen Rouse
Beautiful Machinery - Wendy DeGroat
Odd Mercy - Gail Thomas
The Great Scissor Hunt - Jessica K. Hylton
A Bracelet of Honeybees - Lynn Strongin
Whirlwind @ Lesbos - Risa Denenberg
The Body's Alphabet - Ann Tweedy
First name Barbie last name Doll - Maureen Bocka
Heaven to Me - Abe Louise Young
Sticky - Carter Steinmann
Tiger Laughs When You Push - Ruth Lehrer
Night Ringing - Laura Foley
Paper Cranes - Dinah Dietrich
A Crown of Violets - Renée Vivien tr. Samantha Pious
On Loving a Saudi Girl - Carina Yun
The Burn Poems - Lynn Strongin
I Carry My Mother - Lesléa Newman
Distant Music - Joan Annsfire
The Awful Suicidal Swans - Flower Conroy
Joy Street - Laura Foley
Chiaroscuro Kisses - G.L. Morrison
The Lillian Trilogy - Mary Meriam
Lady of the Moon - Amy Lowell, Lillian Faderman, Mary Meriam
Irresistible Sonnets - ed. Mary Meriam
Lavender Review - ed. Mary Meriam